ATTENTION-DEFICIT
HYPERACTIVITY
DISORDER

ATTENTION-DEFICIT HYPERACTIVITY DISORDER

Juan I. Garcia, M. D.

Rapha Publishing/Word, Inc.
Houston and Dallas, TX

Attention-Deficit Hyperactivity Disorder
by Juan Garcia, M. D.
Copyright © 1991, Rapha Publishing/Word,
Inc., Houston and Dallas, TX

First Printing, 1991
ISBN: 0-945276-28-1
Printed in the United States of America

CONTENTS

THE HYPERACTIVE CHILD AND HIS FAMILY

Attention Deficit Hyperactivity Disorder (ADHD) is a condition which affects approximately three out of every one hundred children in this country. Most of the time the symptoms of this disorder persist throughout childhood, and some studies indicate that up to one third of the children who suffer from ADHD will continue showing signs of it into adulthood. Half of the time this disorder appears before age four, but more often it is recognized when the child enters grade school. There are some indications which show that

ADHD is hereditary, and that it is more common in boys than in girls.

ADHD is a frustrating, frequently ill-defined illness which taxes the resources and patience of an affected child's family. The illness is usually associated with low self-esteem, low frustration tolerance, mood changes, and conduct disorders. Thus, fairly often in their efforts to find help for a child manifesting some or all of these symptoms, a family ends up seeing different specialists and collecting a long list of diagnoses ranging from simple allergies to subtle neurological dysfunctions. The family might also be told that their child is expressing his anger at his parents.

As children with ADHD puzzle most people who work closely with them—from nursery school teachers to Little League coaches—parents may be further confused by teachers, relatives, interested neighbors, co-workers, and even ladies at the supermarket who try to determine what is wrong with the child and suggest various remedies, which might include diets, punishment, discipline charts, etc. Not surprisingly, parents of a hyperactive child find themselves bewildered at this plethora of opinions and find that their time and efforts are increasingly spent looking for a solution to their child's problem and dreading the next call from Junior's teacher.

The first purpose of this booklet, then, is to inform the parents of a child suffering from ADHD of the knowledge we presently have about the illness, some successful treatment options, and the consequences and outcome of the condition. We will explore the different things a family can do to improve the effectiveness of the treatment; that is, how to deal with the school, siblings, and friends of the child. Second, and more importantly, however, we will aim to help the family understand how the ADHD child sees and experiences the world around him: how he tries to keep up with his peers and please his parents and teachers.

Every child, every family, is different. Only you, the parents, can best learn what is a useful or acceptable treatment for your child. That is why we believe that our second objective is the most important. If you become able to identify with your child, to see the world through his eyes, to understand the way he solves his everyday problems, you will be better able to devise creative and useful ways to help him with this disorder.

I have been a child psychiatrist in private practice for over ten years. When people meet me socially and learn about my profession, this kind of conversation usually takes place:

"What kind of problems can children have? I mean, you must see mostly abused children with broken homes and inadequate parents. That must be so hard. I don't see how you can do it."

"Not really," I reply. "I'm very fortunate because most of my patients and referrals come from my neighborhood and church, and I enjoy working with the children and their families very much. Actually, I see a lot of them outside the office, playing in their yards when I walk my dog in the afternoons."

Then they reply in disgust, "Well, I just can't understand, how reasonable parents cannot help their children with their problems. I guess parents don't take the time to take care of their children anymore."

It is difficult for people who haven't encountered ADHD to imagine the frustration, anger, and helplessness that this condition can cause a child and his family. Being a parent is difficult enough, but frustration sets in when a child fails to respond to your efforts or techniques, even though the same techniques may have been successful for your other children (or for your mother-in-law's children who turned out so well). Calls from the teacher or principal, complaints from the parents of a child's friends, reproachful looks in church because a child won't stay quiet during services also engender undue stress in a family. Underlying all these remarks and situations is the muted, or sometimes not so muted, reproach: "Why can't you make your child behave? There's nothing that a little discipline wouldn't solve."

Thus, it is understandable when parents feel inadequate, frequently helpless, or judged and convicted by their peers. In their frustration parents may start blaming each other for being too lenient or too harsh, for working too much or too late, for playing too much golf, for spending too much time on church matters, and the list goes on. Inevitably, their resentment starts centering on the visible source of their troubles, the child. Finally, in resenting the child, his parents struggle against their own feelings, which in turn, causes them feelings of shame and guilt.

Of course, when things get to this point, family counselling is mandatory. Knowing about the illness, understanding the way their child thinks and feels, and realizing that they themselves have had trouble coping with the tensions in their own lives helps the family deal more effectively with the situation. The family is further relieved when they learn that there are medications and other measures to be taken which can improve an ADHD child's condition dramatically. Most important of all, through counselling, parents realize that their child is hurting, confused, terribly unhappy, and despairing of ever pleasing the significant adults (parents, teachers, preachers, coaches, etc.) in his life.

WHAT IS ADHD?

We will begin with a brief historical review of the condition called Attention Deficit Hyperactive Disorder. This condition has been known by several different names since it was first described. When the medical community thought that all hyperactive children had electroencephalographic abnormalities, the condition was called Minimal Brain Dysfunction. It has also been called Hyperkinetic Syndrome, Hyperactivity Syndrome, and Attention Deficit Disorder with Hyperactivity. This frequent change in nomenclature reflects the change in emphasis on what, if anything, medical professionals deem the most important symptoms of the condition, and even now experts cannot agree on many things about ADHD—a sure sign that the condition is still not completely understood. Nevertheless, child experts have been able to identify for several years a particular condition with certain signs and symptoms. Experts now call this condition Attention Deficit Hyperactive Disorder.

Let me clarify a few terms which will aid your understanding of ADHD. First, a symptom is a subjective feeling or sensation described by the patient. Subjective means simply that the feeling is experienced by the patient. For example, a child's complaint that he cannot seem to concentrate as well as his peers may be called a symptom. A sign, on the other hand, is an objective finding. A sign is observed by a person other than the patient. A teacher's observation that a child cannot seem to stay in his chair for a reasonable period of time is a sign. Finally, a syndrome is a cluster of signs and symptoms which consistently appear in a certain condition. And if experts can determine a recognizable cause always present within a syndrome, it may be called an illness.

For many years, pediatricians, child psychiatrists, child psychologists and educators have noticed that certain children seem to manifest some of the same signs and symptoms. For instance, many children are unduly restless and overly impulsive. In addition, these same children tend to be inattentive or have short attention spans; therefore, they are easily distracted, have a tendency to fidget, and an inability to "stay put." They often throw temper tantrums and are prone to moodiness, unusual aggressiveness, and physical complaints such as "nervous stomach," and "nervous headache." One can understand, then, that many of them also have difficulty dealing with their peers.

The problem is that all these complaints can be attributed to a great variety of causes.

For instance, a depressed or angry child may develop all the above mentioned problems. Likewise, children who suffer from some other difficulty, such as a learning disability (dyslexia, for example), may react with similar complaints when confronted daily with an environment in which they cannot seem to achieve success. Again, children with chronic afflictions, such as allergies which obstruct their ability to breathe well or simply to feel well, may also react with tantrums and inattentiveness. What is important to keep in mind is that the syndrome itself can be caused by any of these situations—depression, situational stress, chronic illness, etc. We can consider the possibility that a child is suffering from ADHD only when everything else has been ruled out.

SIGNS AND SYMPTOMS
OF ADHD

The American Psychiatric Association, in the revised third edition of its Diagnostic and Statistical Manual (DSM-III-R) defines ADHD as follows:

A. A disturbance of at least six months during which at least eight of the following things occur:

1. The child often fidgets with hands or feet or squirms in his seat. In adolescents, the symptoms may be limited to subjective feelings of restlessness.

2. The child has difficulty remaining seated when required to do so.

3. The child is easily distracted by extraneous stimuli.

4. The child has difficulty awaiting his turn in games or group situations.

5. The child often blurts out answers to questions before they have been completed.

6. The child has difficulty following through on instructions from others (not due to oppositional behavior or failure of comprehension); for example, the child fails to finish chores.

7. The child has difficulty sustaining attention in tasks or play activities.

8. The child often shifts from one uncompleted activity to another.

9. The child has difficulty playing quietly.

10. The child often talks excessively.

11. The child often interrupts or intrudes on others; for example, he might often butt into other children's games.

12. The child often does not seem to listen to what is being said.

13. The child often loses things necessary for tasks or activities at school or at home—toys, pencils, books, assignments for example.

14. The child often engages in physically dangerous activities without considering possible consequences; however, not for the purpose of thrill-seeking. For example, the child might run into the street without looking for cars.

Note: Consider the criterion met only if the behavior is considerably more frequent than that of most people of the same mental age.

B. The onset occurs before age seven.

C. Does not meet the criteria for a Pervasive Developmental Disorder.

How Can We Tell If Our Child Has ADHD?

In the APA definition, many of the signs and symptoms necessary to make a diagnosis of ADHD are fairly subjective and a matter of individual interpretation. Coming to a diagnosis depends heavily upon the parents' and a teacher's patience and their ability to work with a child.

Typically, the parents' first concern that something may be wrong comes after their child has started school. The reasons for this delay are several: the school requires that the child sit down and listen for long periods of time while remaining relatively understimulated; the child is exposed for the first time to several children his own age and has to learn an increasingly more complicated set of rules; the child is also supposed to be able to follow those rules by himself, without constant encouragement or reminders from the teacher; and, in general, the teachers have a better idea about the normal levels of cognitive development (attention, impulsiveness, memory retention, etc.) than do the parents and can compare the child's behavior with a large sample of children.

Because of all these reasons, the teacher may be the first person to notice that a child may be experiencing some trouble. Frequently, of course, the parents may have already noticed that "Jimmy seems to be a little hyper," but many times the first alarm bell comes from the school.

We Took Our Child To The Doctor....

Once parents have become alarmed, typically, the first stop is with the pediatrician. After listening to the parents' concerns, the doctor will perform a physical examination. With this exam he will rule out allergies, epilepsy, and neurological diseases such as Tourette's Syndrome. He may suggest a diet for the child, but we will talk about that later.

As we saw before, there may be several reasons why the child is acting the way he does. However, if nothing patently wrong is found from a physical standpoint, the pediatrician should, then, refer the child and his family to an expert in child behavior.

He Sent Us To A Psychiatrist

At the psychiatrist's office, this specialist will interview the family and may also interview the child alone. During these interviews he takes careful notes of the family's complaints. Most of the time, particularly in a family where the parents exert reasonable control and discipline, the child will be able to behave fairly well. On the other hand, there are some cases in which the diagnosis is obvious right away, but most often diagnosis is not so easy. If the psychiatrist is reasonably sure that the child's problems are not caused by a problem such as depression or physical ill-health, he may order some tests for the child.

He Ordered Some Tests

These tests are psychological; there are no "lab tests" or "blood tests" for ADHD. Several tests have been devised in order to quantify or estimate such intellectual functions as concentration, impulsiveness, and so on. Some of them are very sophisticated and only a handful of psychologists may have the expertise to give and interpret them. For the most part, however, we have found that we can arrive at a fairly accurate diagnosis with the help of the following simple tests:

1. *Conner's scale.* This is a fairly straightforward questionnaire. It is divided into two parts, one to be answered by the parents and the other one by the teacher. The respondents are asked to evaluate a few parameters and to grade them as "Very much," "Some," "A little," or "Not at all." Typical questions include: "Squirms in his seat," "Runs through his work," and others similar to this.

The answers to the questionnaire are tallied and children with ADHD are supposed to score over a specific number.

2. *Wechsler Intelligence Scale for Children, Revised (WISC-R)*. This is the famous "IQ test." It is composed of twelve tasks which are supposed to measure different components of intellectual capacity. For a child with ADHD, we would expect to find a relative weakness in the tasks that measure concentration, attention span, and attention to detail. (Please note that we are talking about *relative* weaknesses. The child may be extremely intelligent, and the scores in all his tasks may be above average; however, the subscores of tasks that are affected by ADHD would be relatively lower than the others.)

The WISC-R also gives us the best idea about how much we should expect from the child in terms of school performance, but it does not help us pinpoint accurately any learning disabilities. In order to do that we need another test.

3. *Wide Range Achievement Test, (WRAT).* While the WISC-R told us about the native intelligence of the child, the WRAT will tell us how much the child is learning in school. It tests the child's proficiency in reading, writing, and arithmetic and then compares it to a large sample of children from the same grade across the country. Of course, we would expect a very intelligent child to do very well on this test, but that is not always the case. If the child has never gone to school, has had terrible teachers, or is just not working in school, he will tend to test low on the WRAT in spite of high intelligence.

Also, and this is fairly common in children with ADHD, the child may suffer from a learning disability. The learning disabled child is unable, in spite of adequate intelligence and adequate instruction, to perform a task such as reading or writing at the level his intelligence dictates that he should. Obviously, a great degree of frustration results when a smart child finds himself unable to make sense of a written page that his peers can easily skim through.

The *Woodcock-Johnson* and the *Peabody* are a couple of the other achievement tests similar to the WRAT which aid us in determining how well and how much a child is learning in school.

WHAT DO WE DO NOW?

Once we have arrived at a diagnosis, we have a variety of options for treating ADHD. These might include certain diets or medications.

Diet

I have talked to many parents who assure me that they can actually tell when their child has eaten any sugar or artificial dye by the change in the child's behavior, but this has always been a very controversial area in the treatment of ADHD.

In 1975 Dr. Feingold advanced his theory that ADHD, then called hyperactivity, was caused by the presence of artificial substances in the food of American children. There are some problems, however, with his treatment.

First of all, the diet as described by Dr. Feingold is extremely rigorous and difficult to follow. In order to stick to it the parents have to spend hours shopping and preparing dishes from absolute scratch. They must bake bread from special flour, make absolutely sure that any meat that they buy comes from animals that were not given antibiotics, and purchase only vegetables having no trace of fertilizers, etc. Then, of course, they have to live in an area free from air pollution because car exhaust is also included in Feingold's theoretical cause for the disorder.

If the family were to succeed in taking most of the actions mentioned above, (and in my practice I met only one mother who actually made every possible effort to conform to the diet as prescribed by Feingold) then they would have to deal with the tough task of keeping the child on a fairly unpalatable diet without letting him cheat. This action adds to the child's feeling of guilt and anxiety. He feels surrounded by toxic products that will make him "go hyper," and he may also feel that every time he cheats (and cheat he will), he will get what he deserves.

Thus I have always found it interesting that parents who are fairly opposed to medication as a treatment for ADHD sometimes give, as a reason for their reluctance, the fact that their child might feel "different" or "weird" because he has to take a pill. There seems to be little thought for how different or weird a child feels when he sees his peers eating ice-cream, drinking sodas, or eating birthday cake when he is denied them.

Okay, But Does The Diet Work?

Well, it depends on what you read and to whom you listen. The Feingold Institute in

California has published several studies showing that the diet works very well. However, when these same studies were replicated by different researchers at medical schools, the results were consistently negative. Supporters of the Feingold studies claim that the medical researchers are on the payroll of drug companies, and the medical researchers insist that the research done by the Institute is sloppy and based on just a few cases.

My personal opinion is that the Feingold diet and others similar to it ban all sorts of substances without any coherent plan or system. I could understand if they said that some children are unusually sensitive to a particular dye or chemical additive, but it is difficult to think of what all the prohibited substances could have in common and why they would cause this adverse effect on certain children. Also, studies show that some children, who seemed to do much better when the family strictly kept to the diet, continued to do well when researchers introduced several artificial dyes and other proscribed substances into the food without the family's knowledge. Evidently there seems to be a very beneficial effect when the whole family gets involved in a task that the child perceives as in his best interest. This point is extremely important and forms the basis of any successful treatment of ADHD.

What About Sugar?

Once again, several parents have told me that they can tell when their children have eaten sugar; however, the latest medical studies on the subject have failed to reveal that sugar has any effect on behavior. Yet there is a condition known as hypoglycemia, which causes persons suffering from it to experience nervousness, anxiety, and cold sweats after they have ingested moderate amounts of sugar. The condition is much less common than is supposed, and unless a person has an underlying illness, I think that hypoglycemia is rare in childhood.

Again, when children who are supposed to be on sugar-free diets have been observed, the most common finding is that, out of ignorance or temptation, they cheat on their diets. Many adult diabetics, who should be perfectly aware of the consequences, cheat on their diets, so to expect a seven or eight year old child to bypass sugar is, in my view, unrealistic.

So What Do You Do About The Diet?

In my practice, I always take time to discuss diet with the parents. Many times they are very willing to try one, and many of them are fairly adamant about not trying anything else. I always encourage them to give it a try, but I let them know what my experience has been and what my reservations are. If the diet works, I don't argue with the success. Families who are willing to go through that much effort usually, in the long run, prove successful in dealing with all the other problems and difficulties that raising a child with ADHD entails. Nevertheless, my experience has been that, either because the child does not stick to his diet or because the diet just does not work, if a child suffers from a true ADHD, more than dieting is necessary to successfully treat the disorder.

Of course, there may always be the rare case of a child who is definitely allergic to a particular food or substance and reacts to it with hyperactive behavior. Therefore, dieting is always worth a try. And, if a diagnosis is not absolutely clear, medication should be the last resort.

Medication

If medication is deemed necessary to the treatment of the disorder, three types have been found consistently effective in the treatment of ADHD. Let's look at them from least to most effective:

Major Tranquilizers. In pediatric psychiatry the most-used major tranquilizers are haloperidol (Haldol®), chlorpromazine (Thorazine®), and thioridazine (Mellaril®). The basic use of these drugs is for cases of extreme aggressive behavior, or hyperactive behavior which is not responsive to stimulants, or for children with frank neurological problems or mental retardation. The side effects include sedation, muscle stiffness, and dry mouth.

Major tranquilizers should not be used unless other treatments have failed. However, if they are used over long periods of time, these drugs may cause a condition called tardive dyskinesia, an irreversible movement disorder.

Antidepressants. The most commonly used antidepressant for children is imipramine (Tofranil®). Some children respond well to imipramine, for it seems that the drug's beneficial effects are not related to its antidepressant effect. The doses required are smaller than those of other drugs and it takes effect fairly rapidly, which contrasts with the antidepressant effect that may take several weeks to become evident. Imipramine does not have any long-term toxicity (that is, it doesn't leave toxic deposits in the bloodstream), but it does have some side effects. These effects include dry mouth, constipation, dizziness, headaches, and, particularly for the first days of taking it, sedation. Not all children with ADHD respond well to imipramine. Large doses of imipramine (150 to 300 mg) are sometimes used when an antidepressant effect is required. Caution should be exercised with doses of this size because antidepressants may cause cardiac side effects in children.

Stimulants. These are the drugs most commonly prescribed for ADHD. As the name indicates, these drugs produce in most people a feeling of euphoria and increased energy. People using them feel less need for sleep and also experience a decrease in appetite. During World War II, stimulants were used extensively by military personnel who had to go several hours without sleep. Later, in the 1950s stimulants were frequently and generously prescribed for housewives who wanted to lose weight. However, it took the medical world a while to catch on to the fact that these drugs caused addiction and that, when used daily, they made people paranoid and extremely depressed.

You Want To Give This To My Child?

No doctor in his or her right mind would want to give your child something so dangerous. Yet, the truth of the matter is that, for reasons not yet clear, stimulants help children with ADHD. When a child with ADHD takes a stimulant, he experiences a relative "slowing down" of thoughts. While he is working and attending to his lessons, he becomes able to "tune out" most of the things that would otherwise distract him during this time.

I have asked several of the children I see to explain to me how the medication makes them feel. With varying degrees of sophistication, they all tell me a similar story. They are able to stay at their tasks, they do not interrupt as often as before, they take their time instead of rushing through their work, etc. At school, because they can concentrate better and are less fidgety, they do not speak out of turn, pester other children, or play the clown with as much frequency. It is not surprising, then, that teachers usually notice these differences in the children immediately.

There are very few reports of children becoming addicted to stimulants, not even later in adolescence. They can certainly abuse drugs and become addicted to them, but, curiously enough, stimulants do not become the drug of choice.

Let's Take A Closer Look At These Stimulants

Methylphenidate (Ritalin ®). This drug is the most commonly used stimulant. It is easy to use because onset of action is rapid and it is easy to arrive at an effective dose quickly.

The parents notice the effects within half an hour after their child takes the pill.

The drawback to this stimulant is that it lasts only between 4 and 4 1/2 hours, which makes it necessary to give a dose at noon during school. Many children are very sensitive about having to take the medicine and hate to go to the nurse to get the noon dose. Frequently, too, the situation is unconsciously reinforced by one or both of the parents who manage in some way to convey to the child that "you don't need that pill." On the other hand, methylphenidate's short duration of action makes it fairly safe to use and the dosage easy to adjust. If there are any untoward side effects, the parents and child know that the effect will disappear in about four hours.

There is a sustained release form of methylphenidate called Ritalin SR®, and it lasts approximately 7 1/2 hours. This form of methylphenidate can be used when an effective dose has been established. It is more acceptable to parents and children who do not want others at school to find out that they are taking medication.

Side effects to this drug include poor appetite, headache, sedation, nervousness, and abdominal pain. These effects are usually dependent on the dosage. In certain children, stimulants may cause hypertension, so blood pressure should be checked periodically for this reason. It is also not unusual for parents to notice that, while behavior at school improves dramatically, the child appears to be even more "hyper" when he returns home from school. There seems to be a "rebound effect" after the medication wears off. This effect can be easily handled by adding a small dose in the evening at 5:00 or 6:00 p. m.

For a long time there has been concern about the possibility of stimulants slowing down growth. Some studies seem to indicate that some loss in total height (perhaps a couple of inches) may occur in children who have taken stimulants for several years. Other studies have failed to find any significant difference when comparing these children (as young adults) with matching young adults who have never taken the medication. I usually tell the families that there is a chance that the child may fail to grow an inch or two. However, some researchers believe that these effects can be lessened if there is a drug recess during the summer.

Also, there have been reports of children on stimulants who have developed tics (facial grimaces) or even Tourette's Syndrome, a genetic disorder consisting of severe facial and vocal tics which does not usually show up until adolescence or young adulthood. Most researchers seem to think that those children were already suffering from Tourette's, but, once again, it is better to be safe than sorry; the medication should be stopped immediately if the child starts grimacing, squinting, or showing any other repetitive facial movement.

Dextroamphetamine sulfate (Dexedrine®). This was the first stimulant used successfully in the treatment of ADHD. It is still very effective, even for children who have not responded well to methylphenidate. Dexedrine has a longer duration of action than methylphenidate and doesn't lower the seizure threshold, so it would be preferred to methylphenidate when there is a history of seizures. On the other hand, the side effects, though similar to methylphenidate, are more common and this stimulant has a negative "street drug" reputation.

Pemoline (Cylert®). This drug has fewer side effects than Dexedrine® or methylphenidate. Children tolerate it better. It has longer periods of action; thus no noon dose is necessary. The main drawback is that the effect is not evident for several weeks, so it might take a few months to arrive at an effective dose. Also, some children who do well on the other stimulants fail to respond to pemoline.

There is little doubt about the short-term effectiveness of stimulants in the treatment of ADHD. Unfortunately, the long-range benefits have not been that easy to assess. In spite of the fact that the ADHD children who use stimulants do much better behaviorally in the classroom, their grades frequently fail to improve accordingly. Also, researchers have been unable to prove that children with ADHD who were treated with stimulants do much better overall than those who were not treated. We should remember that long term studies are difficult to carry on and that they just reveal general, statistical results; they do not talk about your child. However, this statistical information is important because it tells us that medication alone will not do the trick.

What Are Parents To Expect After Giving A Child Medication For ADHD The First Time?

Ideally, you want your child to feel normal and alert, but I always tell parents that four things might happen. These four things include:

1. Nothing at all happens. The child does not feel any different; you notice no change in his behavior at home or in school. This means that the dose is too low.

2. The child becomes lethargic or sleepy. He complains of feeling "drugged." In this case the dose is too high.

3. The child becomes anxious, shaky, more fidgety and "hyper" than usual. This fact indicates that the child will not do well with stimulants. Do not worry; the side effects will disappear in a couple of hours. For this reason, it is always a good idea to try any new medication on a weekend.

4. The child says he can "think better"; he becomes less moody; his teacher gives a good report; he can tolerate the service at church without the need for you to tie him up. These things indicate that we have found a good dose for the child. At this point we need to work on tightening up the school and home environment, because medication alone will not begin to solve the problems and complications ADHD causes a family.

PUT YOURSELF
IN HIS PLACE

At birth children start learning. They are programed to do so and their capacity for survival depends upon their apprehending and understanding the world around them. A family is a teaching institution, and in its midst a child will be nurtured and protected until his body develops enough for him to take care of himself. Part of this nurturing, of course, is physical, and most families will provide for those needs quite adequately. Just as important, however, parents act as teachers and provide models for how to behave, how to do things, and how society works for their children.

Every child desires to please his parents and make them proud of him. Of course, there are times during which this does not seem to be the case, and the child would certainly deny any desire to please. Nevertheless, in the long run, any child would rather please than displease, be praised than be punished. The same can be said with respect to the child's attitude towards significant adults (adults who are role models such as teachers, preachers, coaches, and relatives). Later, a child also wants to be appreciated and respected by his peers.

Our senses are constantly bombarded by all sorts of stimuli. As I write this paragraph, a bird is chirping outside my window, the neighbor's children have been singing for the last hour and a half, a car is driving down the street, and my legs are beginning to cramp. I could go on forever. So, with all of these distractions, what keeps me concentrating on what I'm doing? Different functions in the brain are constantly busy filtering the stimuli.

Our senses register them but our brain collates and prioritizes them according to the needs of the moment. These filtering functions are the very ones that a child with ADHD has trouble with. He just cannot keep thoughts and sensations from intruding into whatever he is doing at the time, so he loses track faster than his peers. That is why, if you tell him, "Johnny, put on your shoes, pick up the paper, and tell Daddy that Aunt Gladys is here," you will be lucky if he remembers anything about the paper at all.

Of course, an ADHD child with superior intelligence and memory—ability to concentrate is not the same as ability to remember or recall—will do better than a less-gifted child. Still, his performance will not be as good as if he did not have an attention-deficit disorder.

Imagine the problem encountered by the child with ADHD. He is expected, quite naturally, to behave like other children his age, to sit quietly in school, to complete his work on time, to stay quiet in church, and to behave at the table. All these things come naturally to other children his age, but he is unable to do them no matter how hard he tries. Of course, he can try real hard to apply himself, but how long can he hold on to control?

Picture him in the classroom. The teacher is talking or, perhaps, giving out an assignment. Less than a minute after the teacher has given instructions, the child's mind is already wandering, his attention wavering towards the noise that the child behind him makes while writing. He turns around to see what kind of pen his classmate is using. And because children with ADHD tend to be clumsy, he tips his book while turning and it falls on the floor. Of course, the class laughs at him. In order to save his pride, he shoves the desk closest to him or he makes a face at the child in it. The teacher, then, tells him for the umpteenth time to "straighten up, sit down, be quiet, don't fidget." Day after day the ADHD child goes to school only to encounter persistent negative comments from those around him.

Now, picture the child at home. He is bombarded with still more critical comments such as: "I told you to leave the T. V. alone!"; "Let your sister be!"; "Let go of the dog!"; and "What's wrong with you?" Sometimes he may try to help out around the house, but he is all thumbs, and you wish he would stay out of the way. So how can he ever feel that he is pleasing his parents when most of the time he cannot even know that he is in trouble until someone starts complaining?

What To Do About School

Get to know the teacher. When I see a child in consultation, I make a point to call the teacher, tell her that I really appreciate the extra effort she is giving to the child, and I encourage her to call me if she thinks I can be of service to her. Parents, however, should go a step further.

Let her know you care. Not surprisingly, a teacher will be much more sympathetic and patient with your child if she knows that you are going to cooperate with her and that you are interested in what she has to say. Make sure that she feels a part of the treatment team. She will then be more willing to comply with your requirements and needs.

Give the teacher authority. As a rule you should never criticize the teacher in front of your child. Of course, there will be thousands of exceptions, but in general you want to give your child the notion that school is the teacher's realm. Let him know that you will give support at home but you cannot overrule the teacher's authority at school.

Classroom suggestions. Ideally, the child with ADHD should be placed in a classroom with few students. The "open concept" classroom in which several teachers hold their classes in one large room is a disaster for a child with this disorder. I always ask the teacher to put the child's desk in front of the classroom, and, if possible, in front of her desk. This placement minimizes the chances for distractions. For grade school children a system of reward for "good" behavior (tokens, stickers, little toys) can be effective. By rewarding acceptable behavior (staying in one's chair, completing one's work on time), we eliminate some of the unacceptable behavior (getting out of one's desk and roaming around, interrupting work time). The idea is to give the child a chance to be successful and to start associating the classroom experience with something pleasurable by emphasizing what he *can do* rather than what he is *not doing* or what he is *doing wrong.*

What To Do At Home

Obviously the philosophy described above should also be used at home. It is easy to understand how a child's sense of self-worth will receive a boost when he starts feeling that he is finally able to please his parents and teachers predictably and consistently.

Catch the child doing something right! Once you have caught him, reward him. This does not mean you should buy him a portable TV. You may reward him by telling him he did a good job and that you are proud of him. Perhaps Dad could take him out for a hamburger later.

Keep rules constant. Children with ADHD deal very poorly with surprises. They get confused with changes in schedules or plans. If you told him that the family is going to the circus, don't change your mind and go to the movies instead. Similarly, keep schedules as predictable and constant as possible.

Let the child know of any changes in advance. If you do have to change your plans, tell the child beforehand; don't wait until the last minute. Also, it doesn't hurt to remind him gently about appointments: "Tomorrow we go to see your doctor."

Be prepared for sibling rivalry. Children with ADHD tend to be impatient and aggressive. This behavior does not make them particularly endearing or popular with peers or siblings.

At home, brothers and sisters may complain about him at every opportunity. They may use him as a scapegoat to further their own causes in the race for a parent's favor. In school, an ADHD child's peers may avoid him and call him names. His siblings may find this situation embarrassing and even deny any connection with the child. Parents hear comments from brothers and sisters such as, "Mom, why does he act like that? He's such a jerk!"

This predicament is sometimes a no-win situation. It demands all of a parent's patience and ingenuity to keep everybody reasonably happy while still giving the "problem child" the special attention and treatment he requires. A strong sense of family unity solidly established on firm moral principles can make all the difference.

Let him know that he is unique and loved. Scorned by his siblings, usually rejected by his peers, feeling unable to satisfy his parents or teachers, the ADHD child sometimes feels that he is unlovable and worthless. Take time to explain how important he is to you and how special he is to God. Talk to the child about God's love for all creatures, and help him feel His love.

Will It Go Away?

As mentioned before, about a third of the children diagnosed as suffering from ADHD will continue to exhibit some manifestations of it through adulthood. However, natural intelligence, family stability, readily available support, and attention to special needs can make the difference between successful treatment and failure.

The fidgeting, squirming, and clumsiness are the first symptoms to disappear, usually in mid-adolescence. However, the attention deficit may persist. For children who fail to be helped by diet or medication, the prognosis is guarded. Many of them may end up suffering from conduct disorders and engage in delinquent behavior. They are prone to alcoholism and other types of substance abuse. Furthermore, if they fail to achieve some type of academic success before high school, they will most probably fail to finish school.

Therefore, we should place all our efforts into giving these children every possible chance for overcoming their handicap. Working at home and with school, following the recommendations of a specialist you trust, and keeping the family united in the challenge of helping the special child can make all the difference. Family therapy, individual therapy, medication, special studying skills, tutoring and special camps may be required in the treatment of ADHD at some point or another. However, I do not think I need to emphasize that these treatments will have a chance to be successful only in a context of love, respect, and faith.

Editor's note:

At Rapha, we believe that small groups can provide a nurturing and powerful environment to help people deal with real-life problems such as depression, grief, fear, eating disorders, chemical dependency, codependency, and all kinds of other relational and emotional difficulties. The warmth, honesty, and understanding in those groups helps us understand why we feel and act the way we do. And with the encouragement of others, we can take definitive steps toward healing and health for ourselves and our relationships.

Not all groups, however, provide this kind of "greenhouse" for growth. Some only perpetuate the guilt and loneliness by giving quick and superficial solutions to the deep and often complex problems in our lives.

We urge you to find a group of people in your church, or in a church near you, where the members provide acceptance, love, honesty, and encouragement. Rapha has many different books, workbooks, leader's guides, and types of training so that people in these groups can be nurtured in the love and grace of God and focused on sound biblical principles to help them experience healing and growth.

To obtain a free list of the materials we have available, please write to us at:

Rapha, Inc.
8876 Gulf Freeway, Suite 340
Houston, TX 77017

ABOUT THE AUTHOR...

Juan I. Garcia, M.D., is a diplomat of the American Board of Psychiatry and Neurology in General Psychiatry and Child Psychiatry. He specializes in the psychotherapeutic and psychopharmacologic treatment of behavior-disordered children, adolescents, and adults. He is a Clinical Assistant Professor of Psychiatry at Baylor College of Medicine.

Dr. Garcia has been working with Rapha since 1988. For the last two years he has been the Medical Director of the Adult Rapha unit at Sharpstown General Hospital in Houston, Texas.